MW00761470

Self Control

Discover How to Control Your Emotions, Desires, and Behavior through Self Control and Self Regulation

by Francine Edwards

Table of Contents

Introduction

What exactly is self-control? In psychology, it is defined as an individual's ability to control his or her emotions, desires, and behavior to attain some form of "reward" later. Another term for it is 'self-regulation.' Learning self-control is important as it is closely related to one's ability to achieve success in life. Each person has a different concept of success, but whatever that may be – whether it is financial stability or simply happiness – it's guaranteed that self-control is a significant contributing factor.

Despite outward appearances, most people lack self-control in certain aspects of their lives. For example, a student with self-control issues might seem to have everything going for him on the outside, yet he struggles to complete daily homework assignments on time, and when he does, it comes at the price of sacrificing valuable sleep. But the lack of self-control can have a more damaging effect than just missed homework. Adults who experience problems with self-control issues often have difficulties with more important obligations, for example saving money for their future. Or another way a lack of self control can exhibit itself is through the development of destructive habits and dependencies, including substance abuse.

Self-control may seem like an easy concept to apply, but when people are put into the hot seat, they tend to fail. Research shows that when individuals weigh choices, they tend to be logical and reasonable. They carefully evaluate both the long-term and short-term effects of their decisions. But then in reality, as soon as they are in the decision-making stage, they forget all their rationalization. They start to act on impulse by considering the choice that brings about immediate effects. Here's a perfect example: If I asked a woman who's watching her weight whether it's a good idea to eat a slice of cheesecake, she could easily reply that it's not a good idea because although it might taste good for a few minute, that it would set back her weight loss goals and also make her feel guilty afterwards. But then put that same woman in the room with a large slice of cheesecake, and all the rationale behind her earlier commitment starts to fade away. See what I mean?

The good news is, self-control is a *skill* that can be *learned*, and it can actually be *mastered*. It can be developed into subconscious habit through constant practice. Psychological circles also believe that there are many techniques that can be applied to improve one's sense of self-regulation.

In this book, you will learn 13 different techniques that you can apply in order to take control over your emotions, desires, and behavior. Some of the strategies involve taking physical actions, for example regulating your breathing and exercising regularly at critical moments. And others deal with the way you manage your emotions. All of the strategies in this book are easy to understand and apply immediately, so much so that you'll notice your sense of self-control to be already much improved by the end of this book.

© Copyright 2015 by Miafn LLC - All rights reserved.

This document is geared towards providing reliable information in regards to the topic and issue covered. The publication is sold with the idea that the publisher is not required to render accounting, officially permitted, or otherwise, qualified services. If advice is necessary, legal or professional, a practiced individual in the profession should be ordered.

- From a Declaration of Principles which was accepted and approved equally by a Committee of the American Bar Association and a Committee of Publishers and Associations.

In no way is it legal to reproduce, duplicate, or transmit any part of this document in either electronic means or in printed format. Recording of this publication is strictly prohibited and any storage of this document is not allowed unless with written permission from the publisher. All rights reserved.

The information provided herein is stated to be truthful and consistent, in that any liability, in terms of inattention or otherwise, by any usage or abuse of any policies, processes, or directions contained within is solely and completely the responsibility of the recipient reader. Under no circumstances will any legal responsibility or blame be held against the publisher for any reparation, damages, or monetary loss due to the information herein, either directly or indirectly.

Respective authors own all copyrights not held by the publisher.

The information herein is offered for informational purposes solely, and is universal as so. The presentation of the information is without contract or any type of guarantee assurance.

The trademarks that are used are without any consent, and the publication of the trademark is without permission or backing by the trademark owner. All trademarks and brands within this book are for clarifying purposes only and are the owned by the owners themselves, not affiliated with this document.

Chapter 1: Breathing Regulation

Science teaches us that your emotions are your body's way of interpreting physical stimuli. For instance, when you experience an elevated heart rate with sweaty palms and slight nausea before giving an important speech, your brain automatically translates them as signs of anxiousness.

There are many ways to counter these physical responses. When you seek the help of a counsellor, he or she can prescribe you with anti-anxiety medication. A pill can instantly relieve you of unwanted physical stimuli. However, there are easier ways to deal with them. One effective and convenient way is to regulate your breathing. Controlling the way that you breathe may not directly alter your emotions, desires and behavior, but it is one big step in managing them more effectively.

1. Find a quiet place where you can practice your breathing exercises without distraction. Removing the possibility of interruptions (phone and other devices) helps you pay more attention.

2. Sit upright. Sitting is better than lying down. Avoid slouching. When you observe proper posture, the capacity of your lungs to be filled with air is increased.

3. If you are sitting in an arm chair, place your hands on the arm rests. If not, rest them on your lap.

4. For four seconds, inhale slowly through your nose. Your chest and belly should expand as you breathe in.

5. Next, hold your breath for two seconds.

6. Then, for another four seconds, exhale slowly through your mouth. You should not create any noise as you breathe out.

7. Relax for four seconds before you take another breath.

8. Repeat six to eight times. This is the recommended number of breathing cycles to induce feelings of calmness.

It is recommended that you perform this breathing exercise regularly. You can also do it when you have feelings of fear, anxiety and doubt.

Chapter 2: Body Language Adaptation

Our body gestures are more powerful than we think. Not only do they change the way others perceive us, but they also help us feel more in control of our emotions, desires and behavior.

Do a self-check. What kind of body language do you use? Does it show others that you are confident? Or does it give the opposite impression? Altering your body language involves practice and mindfulness. You should be aware of how you act, not only in public but also even when you are by yourself.

1. Always keep a smile on your face. Research proves that when you constantly smile, it can actually make you feel more positive and calm. If you are not smiling, keep your jaw and mouth area relaxed. Clenching your

jaw and pressing your lips together are signs of tension and anger. It may give off the wrong impression to others. Most importantly, it promotes feelings of tension and anger within you.

2. Use body gestures that are "open." Open gestures are the ones wherein your limbs such as your arms are positioned in a free and relaxed manner. These gestures do not require much physical effort. According to researchers, people who use open gestures have higher testosterone levels that causes them to feel more in control.

3. Keep your back straight when you stand and sit but do not apply too much effort that you look tense. Position your feet shoulder-width apart from each other and distribute your weight evenly throughout your body. Avoid making unnecessary movements, like fidgeting and wiggling.

4. Make eye contact when you speak to others. Refrain from looking into the distance when you communicate. When you look at other people directly in the eye, it conveys that you are assertive and in charge of yourself. It also makes others feel that you are eager to listen to them.

5. Move smoothly and calmly. Do not be fidgety. If you are not careful with the way that you move, it gives people the impression that you are childish or immature. Also avoid distasteful gestures like pointing and staring.

Chapter 3: Enhancing Your Endorphins and Your Attitude

Your emotions are controlled by chemicals in your body called hormones. Feelings of stress, for example, are caused by high levels of cortisol. But not all hormones cause negative emotions. There are some that are considered as natural mood boosters. Endorphins belong to this category and their production is induced when you are physically active. Have you ever heard of someone who is in a bad mood and decides to go for a run? Believe it or not, running actually helps because it stimulates the production of feel-good hormones.

Exercising is also more than just promoting hormone production. Being physically active helps you develop a positive attitude. A number of studies have discovered that people who are physically active are more energetic and positive. They also feel more in control of their lives.

The most common problem that people have related to exercise is that they feel that they don't have time for it. Exercising regularly should not take too much of your time daily. You can incorporate exercise into your daily routine.

1. Exercise for 15 minutes in the morning. Go for a short run. If running is too physically stressful for you, try brisk walking. If you have a pool at home or if you live near a facility that has a pool, aim for a few laps. Do yoga. Perform a quick exercise routine or do household chores such as cleaning your car and mowing your lawn.

2. Enroll yourself in a physical fitness gym. Working with an instructor and a specific exercise program teaches you the value of discipline and commitment. Both are essential in improving your self-control.

3. Join competitive sports. Are you good in a particular kind of sport? Or would you like to learn how to play one? Grab the opportunity. Search for teams in your community or workplace that you can join. Participate in sports workshops. Participating in competitive sports not only improves your physical health, it also provides you with a way to set and achieve goals. When you finish a marathon or win in a sports league, your success enhances your feeling of being in charge of yourself.

Chapter 4: Giving Yourself a Break

When you are overthinking, your brain works like a broken record. You tend to think about the same things over and over again. Your thoughts run wild and eventually, you lose control over them.

Many people engage in overthinking because they feel that it helps them solve their problems. It doesn't. It only makes the situation worse. When you are overthinking, you are simply wasting your time and effort. You are also training yourself to be controlled by your thoughts and impulses.

If you catch yourself overthinking, there are many ways that you can snap out of it. One of the simplest ways is to give yourself a break. Changing your environment, even just for a short while, can help ease your mind, which is a big step if you want to regain control of your emotions, desires and behavior.

Taking a break does not exactly mean packing up your suitcases and heading over to an exotic destination for a holiday. Taking a break can simply mean resting your mind for two minutes. Researchers discovered that even just a two-minute break can create a positive effect within you.

For short breaks that range from five minutes to half an hour, you can enjoy a meal with a friend or co-worker. Read a book. Talk to someone. Take a quick nap. Go for a fifteen-minute run. You can do a lot in a short period of time. Choose the activities that you engage in wisely. Perform activities that are positive and wholesome. Involving yourself in destructive practices will not help you learn self-control.

If you can take longer breaks that last an hour or two, you can step out and enjoy a relaxing walk at the park. Play with your pet. Exercise or play a sport of your choice. Take your significant other on a date. Spend quality time with family. Catch a movie that you've always wanted to watch.

Breaks that take weeks and months are great for you when you are under a great amount of pressure. If you have the luxury of time, use it to do something meaningful like acquire a new skill. Travel to places that you have always wanted to visit. Visit relatives and friends that you haven't communicated with for a long time. Perform community service. The options are practically endless.

Chapter 5: Rewiring with Meditation

Meditation is a method that works on a spiritual level. It rewires your brain, increases your self-awareness and puts into perspective a lot of important things that you may have missed. It changes the way that you respond to stressful situations and people. Meditation trains you to be calm and relaxed despite unfavorable circumstances. Additionally, meditating for at least 20 minutes a day also contributes to your physical health. It is a great habit that you should develop if you want to enhance your self-control.

There are many kinds of meditation that you can learn. You can find them as you browse through various sources, such as books and internet articles. If you know a practitioner, you can also ask them for tips, advice and guidance.

Technology makes it convenient for you to learn meditation. There are online sources like YouTube that offer guided meditations. You can download and use them daily. For instance, MIT's website offers meditations that concentrate on promoting relaxation and mindfulness. Do not hesitate if you are a beginner. Meditation is quite easy to learn.

1. Find a quiet place. Keep distractions to a minimum when you meditate. Concentration is important if you want to experience optimal results.

2. Sit down comfortably. Observe proper posture. Then, close your eyes.

3. Focus on your breathing. Breathe slowly with your nose for four seconds. Hold your breath for two to three seconds. Release your breath with your mouth for another four seconds. Repeat this breathing exercise until you feel calm and relaxed.

4. Keep your eyes closed. Breathe slowly with your nose for four seconds. With conviction, recite this mantra: "I am in control." Then breathe out with your mouth for four seconds. Repeat five times.

5. To conclude your meditation, gradually come to your awareness. Remind yourself of the present moment. Feel your body—your head, arms, fingers, legs and toes. When you have come to your senses, slowly open your eyes.

Chapter 6:   Progressive Muscle Relaxation

Progressive Muscle Relaxation is a technique that involves a two-step process that lowers your tension and stress levels. This exercise is particularly helpful when you feel that you are losing control. When your emotions, desires and behavior get out of hand, you may feel a series of physical manifestations. Negativity often manifests itself in the form of body pain—neck pain, shoulder pain, headache, you name it. Progressive Muscle Relaxation relieves body pain and by extension, helps you gain better control of your emotions, desires and behavior. When your body is relaxed, you can think more clearly and feel more in control.

People who lack self-control generally feel tense throughout the day. They are so tense that they cannot identify what relaxation actually feels like. By practicing Progressive Muscle Relaxation, you train your body to recognize the difference of a tensed muscle from a relaxed one. When you have learned to distinguish the two, you can use muscle tension as a warning signal that you are starting to lose control over yourself. This improves your awareness.

1. Spare 15 minutes of your time. Find a quiet and relaxing space that is free from distractions.

2. Sit down. Do not slouch. Observe proper posture but do not overdo it. Your back should be straight but should feel relaxed. If you are wearing tight clothing, loosen them or take them off. Begin breathing deeply then close your eyes.

3. Identify your tense muscles and focus on them. For example, your target muscle group is located at the area around your forehead. Take a deep breath and squeeze the muscles in that particular area as hard as you can. In the example, since the muscles are located around your forehead, try squeezing them by moving your eyebrows. Hold for five minutes and slowly release. Be careful as you observe this step. Beginners may accidentally cause

tension to other muscles but with practice, you will get better.

4. Relax for 15 seconds. Proceed to the next muscle group that you want to work on.

5. If you have finished working on all tense muscle groups, relax for about ten to fifteen minutes before you open your eyes.

Chapter 7: Practicing Self-Awareness

In order to control your emotions, desires and behavior, you need to recognize them first. Too often, people find it difficult to manage themselves because they cannot notice the patterns that their emotions, desires and behavior take. They are in denial. Developing self-awareness can be complicated at first, but with constant practice, you can learn it.

Strive to keep a daily journal. Record your day to day experiences and most importantly, write down your feelings. Do not simply write down the emotion that you have felt. Also indicate the reasons that caused you to feel that way. Do not write, "I got angry at work today." Elaborate. Write down, "I got angry at work today because my boss rejected my proposal. I had worked hard on it. I spent weeks polishing it to make sure it got approved."

At the end of every week, read what you have recorded in your journal. Make an evaluation of your feelings. Be aware of what made you happy, sad or upset. Find patterns in your emotions, desires and behavior. As often as possible, write in your journal every day.

Another thing that you can do is to spend a portion of your time contemplating on your emotions, desires and behavior. In between your busy schedule, cram in some minutes to think. You can do it as you wake up in the morning or before you sleep at night. You may even do your thinking when you are having your afternoon coffee at your office's cafeteria or staffroom.

Question yourself. When was the last time that you felt strongly about something? Then ask yourself why you felt that way. For instance, if you recall that you have been feeling gloomy the whole week, analyze why. Is it because you had a fight with your significant other? What caused that fight? Did your behavior cause that fight? If so, what can you do to change that behavior? Look at every angle and always seek to improve your control over yourself. Do not simply indulge yourself in a whirlwind of thoughts. Think with a purpose in mind.

Chapter 8: Preoccupation with Humor

Humor works like a wall between you and your uncontrollable emotions, desires and behaviors. It cools you down before you start acting on impulse. It relaxes your mind before you begin to overthink. Most importantly, humor has a positive effect on your behavior. People who can find humor even in unfavorable situations are optimistic, positive and in control.

Humor also keeps your mind preoccupied with a positive thought. When you are upset or unhappy, negativity seeps into your mind which in turn, causes you to feel impulsive emotions and entertain irrational thoughts. That is when you begin to lose control. But when you try to find something to laugh about, you leave no room for negativity.

For example, you may feel embarrassed when you make a slip-up during your big speech at work. Everybody starts laughing at you. If you allow your emotions to overcome you, you will have a hard time coping with the incident. You may start to feel small about yourself. However, if you laugh at your own slip-up, your little mistake won't seem so bad. People will also deem you as a good sport. Laughing at your own slip-up creates a good impression, rather than panicking over it.

Humor is useful when you feel that anger is about to rule you. When someone or something upsets you, it's easy to give in to your emotions. Before you lose control, change your perspective right away. Find something to laugh about. When your children make a mess, do not give in to anger right away. Laugh it off. When your boss ignores the report that you worked hard for, do not let yourself be enraged. Laugh it off. Develop humor as a habit and you will start seeing things from a brighter perspective.

Chapter 9: Developing Gratitude

When you express your gratitude to someone, you are not only showing appreciation to the other person. You are also doing yourself a favor. You are helping yourself develop the value of gratitude, which helps you feel more in control. You may not know it but studies show that frequently expressing your gratitude lowers stress levels. When you feel less stressed, you can think better and thus, be more in control of your emotions, desires and behavior.

Count your blessings. Make a "gratitude list." Take a piece of paper and write down every single thing or person that makes you feel grateful. Are you grateful for your family? Are you grateful for being awarded a promotion at work? Are you grateful that you brought an umbrella to work today? Recall both the big and little things. Make sure to write them all down. When you are done, read the list that you created. This practice will remind you that you have a lot to be grateful for.

You can keep the list somewhere private, like in your journal; and when you feel stressed or unhappy, take out that list and read it to yourself. It should boost your mood. Another option is to keep it in a place where you can often see it. You can hang it on your fridge door or post it on your daily planner to serve as a constant reminder.

A simple way to cultivate the habit of gratitude is by frequently expressing your "thank you" to people who have helped you. Whether they did a small or big gesture for you, do not fail to show them your gratitude. If your spouse made you a delicious meal, compliment him or her and say "thank you." If your co-workers helped you prepare a report, do not forget to let them know that you are grateful.

Your gratitude should not only be reserved for people who have done something nice for you. You should also teach yourself to be grateful even for difficult situations and people. For instance, it is hard to be grateful if you got fired at work. Who loves losing a job anyway? As difficult as it is, find an angle that you can work with. For example, you can say, "I am still grateful even if I lost my job. This way, I can spend more time with family" or "I am still thankful even if the company let me go. I have met amazing people who have become my mentors. I also had a lot of learning opportunities. This is my chance to use what I have learned to find myself a better job."

Chapter 10: Therapeutic Talking

Talking about your emotions, desires and behavior has a lot of benefits. It increases your self-awareness and helps you sort out complicated thoughts. Studies also show that venting has a therapeutic effect on the human brain.

When your mind is "crowded" with thoughts, you tend to lose control over your emotions, desires and behavior. You snap back at people. You feel stressed out. Talking to someone may not solve your problem, but it helps you figure out the solution. It helps you feel positive as you go through your dilemma.

If you feel troubled, do not react immediately. If you have to make a difficult decision, do not give in to your impulsive desires. Talk to someone that you trust first. Discussing your feelings and desires with someone else may put some important things into perspective. The opinions of others can help you make the right choice.

If someone angered you, do not fight back with harsh words or physical violence. Bad behavior will not benefit you at all. Instead, talk to the other person. Settle matters like an adult. Be calm and choose positive words.

You can start cultivating this habit by gradually opening up to the people around you. You can begin at home. Share positive news and experiences with your family. Interact with them over meals. At breakfast, tell them about your plans for the day. At dinner, tell them about what happened during your day. If you live by yourself, you can always call other people. Talking to the people that you work with is also a great idea.

The most common misconception is if you talk to a mental health professional, you have mental problems. Do not let this myth hinder you. Seeing a counselor or therapist helps you understand and control your emotions, desires and behavior. Find a mental health professional that you are comfortable working with. Consider someone whom you feel that you can open up to.

Chapter 11: Focusing on the Future

When we are emotional, we lose sight of reality. We are so consumed by our emotions that we become ungrounded. In this situation, the biggest challenge is to remind yourself of the consequences of your actions. "What would my anger cause if I acted on it?" "What opportunities would I lose if I let my sadness overcome me?" By asking yourself these questions, you remind yourself that your emotions are just temporary. Understanding that feelings are only short-lived helps you control them.

While you are in the moment, you may feel overwhelmed. It may seem that you have a storm of emotions within you. It may be difficult to understand how you feel, but in order to manage your emotions, desires and behaviors, you have to step back and contemplate. Separate your feelings from what you are actually experiencing. Most likely, you are just putting a magnifying glass on your emotions.

Take this situation, for example: You are on the way home after a long day at work. You feel stressed out and as you drive home, you can't stop wishing for time to go faster. Suddenly, a car from your right crashes right into your vehicle. You're not harmed, but your brand new SUV is in bad shape. The driver of the other car steps out of his vehicle to approach you. He looks apologetic. In this situation, it is tempting to get mad and hurt the other person either physically or with hurtful words. But before you give in to your emotions and your desire to inflict instant damage on the other person, take a step back. What are your feelings? You feel extremely angry. You feel stressed. You feel frustrated. What is actually happening? Someone accidentally bumped into your car. Evaluate your reaction. Is your reaction appropriate? Are you overreacting to the situation?

Meanwhile, if anxiety is the problem, focusing on the future also helps. Think about how you will feel in the future if you handle your current situation poorly. For instance, if you feel anxious about presenting an important proposal at work, think about how it may affect your career. Is it going to gain you a promotion if you do it successfully? If you fail, how small will it seem after a couple of months?

Chapter 12: Challenging the Urge to Catastrophize

Pessimists have the habit of "catastrophizing." They always assume the worst in everything. When you catastrophize, your thoughts spin out of control and you feel anxious. For instance, a catastrophizing thought about getting your proposal rejected at work could go like this: "The boss rejected my proposal. My boss doesn't like me. I am a failure. I am pretty sure that in a month's time, I will be jobless."

Stop yourself from being pessimistic by challenging yourself when you catastrophize. If you catch yourself jumping to conclusions, ask yourself for evidence that supports your presumptions. Your proposal got rejected. Is it possible that your boss rejected it because your company doesn't have the budget to accommodate more projects at the moment? Possibly! If your boss doesn't like you, can you get fired for it? Is there a possibility to lose your job over a rejected proposal? There are labor laws that protect your rights as an employee. Your superiors cannot fire you without just reasons. Be logical and most of all, be realistic.

Pessimistic people also practice "filtering." They love to focus on the negative side of a situation which is why they often fail to see the positives. Pessimists see things in black and white. A situation can only either be good or bad. It is all or nothing. There is no "in-between." An example of filtering would be assuming that the whole day is going to be a disaster just because you had a flat tire that morning.

You can fight filtering by making yourself understand that there is such a thing as middle ground. Recognize that things do not need to be perfect. Sometimes, a situation can be imperfect and still turn out great. So what if you had a flat tire? Tell yourself: "I am not going to let this flat tire ruin my day. I can still be productive."

Chapter 13: Removing Yourself from Personalization

When we are overwhelmed by our emotions and desires, we tend to personalize. What exactly is personalization? It happens when we think that the actions of others are either targeted against us or a direct response to us. It is a way of thinking where we feel that everything seems to revolve around us. When we personalize, we feel paranoid, as if other people have intentions to "get us." Our mind is filled with outrageous and overwhelming thoughts. This increases our chance of spinning out of control.

To have a full grasp of what personalization is, imagine yourself sitting at your office desk. Your co-worker is walking past with an angry expression on his face. As he passes by your desk, he accidentally knocks over the stack of documents that you have on the edge of the table. You immediately assume that he is mad at you so you do your best to avoid him during meetings and other office gatherings.

You can beat personalization by empathizing with others. Put yourself in their shoes so that you can understand them better. Recognize the fact that they too are human beings with emotions, just like you. Use your brain, be logical. Your co-worker may have had a bad day. Because he was in a hurry to get out of the office, he knocked over the stack of documents on your table. Another factor that you should consider is that you placed the stack right at the edge of your desk. By placing it there, there is a greater likelihood for someone to accidentally knock it over.

If rationalizing with yourself doesn't calm you down, the best way to challenge personalization is to ask the other person directly. Ask them about what is actually going on and you will be relieved to know that it has absolutely nothing to do with you.

Conclusion: Applying What You Have Learned

Your emotions and desires are not bad. When kept under control, our emotions motivate us to create a lot of positive things. They encourage us to go out of our comfort zones, connect with other people and savor the good things in life. Likewise, our desires are also powerful motivators. Because of them, we learn to set interesting goals and strive to accomplish them.

Imagine a person without emotions and desires. That individual can be compared to a boring rock. His life has no excitement or color. He remains stagnant and dull. So don't shun your emotions and desires as though they were illnesses. An adequate amount of them is actually healthy for us. Your main goal should be to learn how to master both. With the different methods discussed in this book, you can gradually develop self-control.

Remember, self-control does not happen overnight. You don't just wake up one day already an expert at managing your emotions, desires and behavior. It takes time and effort to get a hold of yourself. Do not feel discouraged if you make some mistakes along the way. Just be persistent and, in time, you will begin to feel amazing results.

Finally, I'd like to thank you for purchasing this book! If you found it helpful, I'd greatly appreciate it if you'd take a moment to leave a review on Amazon. Thank you!

35310591R00039

Made in the USA
Middletown, DE
27 September 2016